The Castles of Gower

The Gower Society

First published in 1970 by
The Gower Society
c/o Swansea Museum, Victoria Road
Swansea, SA1 1SN

Reprinted 1973, 1976
Revised edition 1985, 2005

ISBN 0-902767-35-6

Printed in Wales by
Dinefwr Press, Rawlings Road
Llandybie, Carmarthenshire, SA18 3YD

Introduction

The Normans seized Gower from its Welsh ruler shortly after 1100 A.D. The ancient Welsh Commote of Gŵyr, extending from the peninsula northwards to the Amman Valley, became henceforth the Norman "Lordship of Gower" and the best land in the Lordship was parcelled out into numerous manors. The Norman seizure did not pass unchallenged, and counter attacks from the independent Welsh states to the north and west continued throughout the next two centuries. As a defence against these attacks, the new masters of Gower erected castles in many of their manors.

These early castles were not the towering stone structures we see today, but were formed of great banks of earth and rubble stone thrown up to enclose an oval or circular courtyard, in which stood the hall of the new lord of the manor. Castles of this type bore the brunt of the frequent Welsh attacks, and the Welsh chronicles joyfully record their occasional capture. The Welsh successes were temporary, and most of the castles were repaired and re-fortified as soon as the Welsh had withdrawn.

A fine example of one of these early castles can be seen on the southeast tip of Penmaen Burrows, overlooking Three Cliff Bay. Here, excavations by Leslie Alcock in 1960 revealed that the entrance, through the rubble bank, had been surmounted by a great timber tower. Two buildings had stood in the courtyard, one of timber, the other a large and crudely constructed stone structure. The massive timbers of the gate tower survived as charred stumps, and these and the fire-reddened soil in the adjacent rampart provided graphic evidence for the success of one Welsh attack in the peninsula.

An earlier archaeological venture in 1898 at Barland Castle, near Bishopston, found in the earthen bank around the site the clear imprint of a row of timber stakes, the remains of a strong palisade which had once sheltered the new lord of Bishopston.

The largest of these early castles is the huge, oval mound at Penrice village, known as the "Mounty Bank", or, more prosaically, as "Penrice Old Castle" (there are several other lesser examples of this type of castle to be found elsewhere in Gower). The more conventional pudding-basin shaped motte castle is quite rare in this area, but an example survives at Llandeilo Talybont (near Pontarddulais).

Swansea Castle had either a motte or a ringwork, though the experts disagree. Whichever it was, it stood midway between the present stone castle and Welcome Lane. This feature is shown in eighteenth century views of Swansea, and traces of it were found during building works on the site in 1913. Swansea Castle was the principal castle of the Lordship of Gower, and appropriately it was the largest, though little of it now survives.

The stone castles with which we are more familiar did not begin to take shape until the middle of the thirteenth century, and the greater part of their curtain walls and towers were erected at the end of that century. In 1282, Llewellyn "the Last" had been killed in battle, and most of the warfare in Gower was over. The stone castles impress us now, but it was their more simple predecessors which played the greater part in the centuries of warfare between conquerors and dispossessed in Gower.

Penrice, Pennard, Oystermouth, Weobley and Swansea are all stone castles dating mainly from the end of the thirteenth century. Oyster-mouth, second only in importance to Swansea, was a favoured country seat of the lords of Gower, and the architectural embellishment of this fine building was carried out in the early part of the fourteenth century. Weobley was a strongly fortified manor house, rather than a true castle, and within its walls, the great hall, kitchen and private rooms are still easily identified. Oxwich is a late version of Weobley: rebuilt completely in Tudor times as a palatial mansion, but soon abandoned by the wealthy Mansels for their more convenient residence at Margam Abbey.

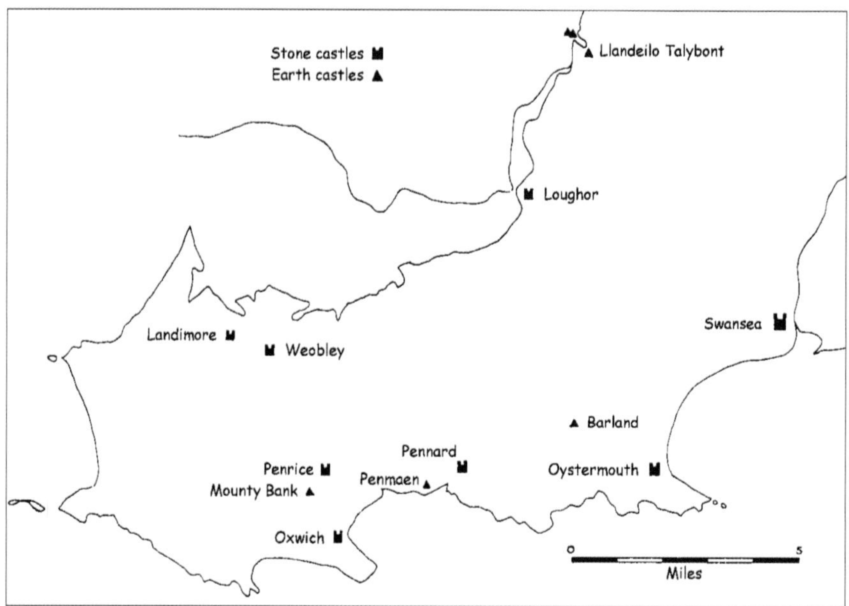

The stone and earth castles of Gower.

Penmaen Castle, c.1130 AD.
(Reconstruction by Michael Gibbs 1969, based on excavations by Leslie Alcock in 1960).

Penmaen Old Castle

The early Gower castles of the first years of the conquest bore little resemblance to later versions. However, they were not the hastily constructed, flimsy and temporary structures that some people imagine. A castle was built in a strong position on Penmaen Burrows in the twelfth century. It consisted of a massive encircling bank of limestone rubble fronted by a deep rock-cut ditch. Even today, the ditch and steep rampart present a formidable obstacle. Excavations in 1960 revealed traces of a large timber gate-tower, which had been destroyed in an intense fire. After this destruction, the entrance was made much narrower, and the tower was not rebuilt, but a large and crudely built stone hall was erected on the seaward side of the site. The artist's reconstruction shows both these phases of the castle's history. The site was abandoned before the mid thirteenth century, and so was never concealed below a later stone castle, as happened so often elsewhere.

Swansea Castle: Buck preliminary version for print published in 1741 (detail).

The Old Castle at Swansea

The first castle at Swansea was a simple, but strong, embanked enclosure, formed of rubble and earth with timber or rubble stone breast-works. It covered an area of around 1.85 hectares (4.6 acres) on and to the north of the New Castle site. Part of its site is now occupied by the buildings which form the east side of Castle Street. When these buildings were erected in 1913, extensive traces of the old castle were revealed and destroyed in the digging of basements and foundations. It could then be seen that at least two succeeding phases of castle building had occurred on the site. Initially there was a ringwork or motte, which was first recorded in 1116, when it was attacked and the outworks fired by Gruffudd ap Rhys.

This early castle suffered at the hands of the Welsh on several occasions, and the 1913 excavations revealed quantities of fire-damaged rubble in the lowest filling of the ditch. Sometime in the early thirteenth century, the castle was re-fortified with mortared stone walls. These consisted of a curving curtain wall, with at least one very massive square projecting tower. This may have been the castle destroyed by Llewellyn the Great in 1215.

The illustration is part of a print of 1741 by Samuel and Nathaniel Buck. It shows the "New Castle" much as it is today. In the centre of the picture just above the ship's masts can be seen a tree-surmounted mound and perhaps the original ringwork or motte which marked the site of the "Old Castle".

Swansea Castle from Castle Square.   *Northeast square tower from The Strand.*

The New Castle at Swansea

At the end of the thirteenth century, a large fortified block of domestic buildings was erected immediately to the south of the war-torn "old castle" at Swansea. The new block contained a spacious great hall with private apartments at the east end, and provision for kitchens at the other. The supposed kitchen wing has now been destroyed, but the fine first-floor hall and adjacent private rooms have survived. Sometime before 1347, the rather plain hall was ornamented by the addition of the fine arcaded parapet, which still forms the castle's most striking feature. This work is possibly attributable to John, Lord Mowbray, who succeeded to Gower in 1331. These graceful arches are similar to those added by Bishop Henry de Gower to his palaces at St. David's, and to Lamphey in Pembrokeshire.

The town was visited by King Richard 11 in May 1399 when he was en route to Ireland, at which time the castle may have been in a neglected condition. The castle was prepared for defence in the Civil War, but apparently saw no action. After that it served a variety of purposes and before 1678, a flourishing glass works had been established there, with its furnaces within the detached square tower. It produced squat black wine bottles. Traces of this glass works were found during restoration work.

In 1957, plans were mooted to demolish the castle to make way for redevelopment, but happily not pursued. Its last commercial tenant was the *South Wales Evening Post*. On their leaving, in 1968, the print-works and offices were removed, the ancient walls were consolidated and the surroundings landscaped.

The arcading added in the fourteenth century.

The arcading: detail.

Southwest tower showing gun-loops for mortar (mid 1400s).

Oystermouth Castle.

Oystermouth Castle

Within a short time of the conquest of Gower, Oystermouth Castle came into the hands of the chief lord of Gower, and was held by him jointly with Swansea Castle. The Welsh Chronicles record the destruction of a castle which was probably that of Oystermouth: "there was a castle in Gower which he (Gruffydd ap Rhys ap Tewdwr) burnt entirely killing many men therein". This invasion into Gower took place in 1116. The site was re-fortified, but the castle was burned again in 1216. The central block of buildings forming the present keep took its present form during the thirteenth century during the lordships of William de Braose II and III, but parts of it may date from the twelfth century. In 1284, Edward I stayed at Oystermouth for two nights during his progress through Wales following the death of Llewellyn the Last. In 1287, the castle was extensively damaged in a final outbreak of warfare, part of a violent campaign by one of the King's former Welsh allies.

In the late thirteenth and early fourteenth centuries, Oystermouth seems to have been the preferred residence for the lords of Gower, rather than Swansea, and most of the remains seen today took their present form when the damage of 1287 was repaired. The concave faces each side of the gateway are the internal remains of round towers which may have flanked the entrance. Evidence suggests, however, that the towers were planned, but probably never built. The most graceful work is to be seen in the tall chapel tower, with its great buttresses and delicate tracery. This was added in the early fourteenth century when the castle had become a favourite residence of the de Mowbray family. George Grant Francis was responsible for restoration and the reconstruction of much of the chapel block's 'window' tracery in the 1840s. The castle had a pigeon house, similar to those at Oxwich and Penrice; it was located some 70 yards N.E. of the castle, but destroyed in the early twentieth century.

Oystermouth Castle: Gateway.

One of the gateway towers.

Oystermouth Castle: The chapel.

Pennard Castle from the golf course.

Pennard Castle

Pennard is the most impressive of the Gower castles when seen from the valley to the north, and on this side, the curtain wall is almost intact. Until stone defences were built around 1300, Pennard Castle was probably a palisaded ring-work. On the windward side, the greater part has collapsed (some in 1961) and some repairs were later carried out. The twin gate towers are simple but attractive, and with most of the visible remains, date from the end of the thirteenth century. Within the be-sanded courtyard, the rounded corners of the hall are sometimes visible. Excavations in 1961, exposed the greater part of this twenty metre long building. Although only two courses or so of stonework remained, the hall was a text-book example of its type with a private room for the lord, the main room with its hearth, and two service rooms beyond the entry. By abutting the outside of the curtain wall, its 7.5m. square tower saved on internal space – this appears to have been for residential purposes, and is constructed on a rock base. By 1650, the castle was already be-sanded and desolate, and a print of 1741 shows it much as it appears today.

Pennard Castle in the snow.

Pennard Castle showing the limestone and sandstone layers.

Penrice Old Castle

As with Penmaen Castle, this site was fortified in the early years of the conquest, but was never disturbed by the building of a later castle. It was probably abandoned when the first mortared stone castle of Penrice was built just over half a mile to the N.E. in the mid thirteenth century. This is the biggest of the early castle ringworks in Gower, as befits the rich manor of Penrice. The site has not been excavated, but the extensive and high defensive banks indicate that this was a complex and important castle, known as the 'Mounty Bank' or 'Mountyborough'. The site is now much overgrown, and although it stands so near to Penrice village, it is easily missed by the casual traveller. Yet, when one looks at the bulk of these heaving ramparts, it is apparent that these early castles were formidable defences, erected with great labour, and well suited to the warfare of the time. It is likely to have been built by a member of the Penres family from Devon, but was abandoned in favour of the new one to the N.E.

Penrice Castle

Sir Robert de Penres, in the early 14th century, is the first lord of Penrice to be clearly identified by records. In 1410, the death of Isabella de Penres led to the succession of both Oxwich and Penrice passing to her husband, Hugh Mansel. Penrice remained the seat of the Mansel family until they abandoned it in favour of Oxwich.

The site was probably chosen because of the limestone outcrops on which it is built – on three sides they form an excellent natural defence. It is the largest of the Gower castles, but contains few buildings. It consists of a single-walled irregular hexagon, its shape dictated by the site. The crude stonework was held together well by good local mortar. The earlier mortar was brown and sandy, whereas the later mortar showed as a distinctive limey white. These mortars help to define the two main periods of building activity.

The principal group of towers and apartments stood along one wall, facing the only level approach to the castle. Here, there is a small round keep of three storeys, the oldest surviving part of the castle. Attached to this are the remains of the hall of the castle, with a porch added later. Nearby are two fragmentary towers, said to have been destroyed by gunpowder, to make the castle indefensible after the Civil War. Two similar towers, flat-fronted with rounded corners, form the gateway. Apart from the keep, which was built in the mid 13th century in a crude form but with

Penrice Castle gatehouse.

walls 2.2m. thick, most of the visible stonework at Penrice dates from the end of that century. The curtain wall has few defensive features except for a series of small solid half-round towers or bastions.

Little was added after the 13th century, apart from a well-preserved stone pigeon house (dovecote) outside the south-east wall, which was added by 1534, and was a late work of the Mansels. It probably replaced a bastion, and has a narrow doorway to the S.W. It is beehive-shaped, rounded, rising to a domed roof with no external wall holes. The dome has a central entrance/exit hole and nest holes line the interior walls. Agricultural demands in the 19th century led to some buildings, of a rather rough and ready nature, which were set inside the castle grounds, against the curtain wall.

The somewhat austere 'new' Penrice Castle, set in extensive landscaped grounds, was designed by Keck (who also designed Highgrove, home of the Prince of Wales) and built in the 1770s. The pseudo medieval gateway towers were added some twenty years later. Penrice is privately owned and occupied by descendents of the same family that built the original castle.

Penrice Castle gatehouse from the interior.

Penrice Castle on its rocky bluff.

Penrice Castle west tower and curtain wall.

Penrice Castle curtain wall.

17

Oxwich Castle

During the first half of the 16th century, Sir Rice Mansel, soldier and Crown Officer, rebuilt as a vast mansion house, the castle in which he was born. An impressive crested gateway (the heraldic plaque bears his initials), flanked by solid drum turrets, gives access to a courtyard. Opposite the gateway, a long-destroyed three-storeyed porch contained a staircase which led to the huge first floor. One of the windows of this hall is still clearly visible, and traces of a narrower, taller window, which lit the dais on which the lord took his meals can also be made out. Over the whole of this block, ran what may have been a long gallery, one of the earliest of its kind. The window openings of the 'gallery' indent the top of the present ruins. At the family end of the house, a fine stair gave access to this floor, but at the service end, a similar staircase stopped short at the floor below.

A stone pigeon house, similar to that at Penrice, stands nearby, close to some fragments of an earlier castle incorporated into the new building. The two-storey range on the south of the courtyard is slightly later than the main block, which it abuts.

By 1580, the Mansels had decamped to their new home at Margam Abbey. An undocumented early ring-work, possibly built by the de la Mares in the twelfth century, has been identified at Norton, half a mile N.W. of the present castle.

Oxwich Castle chimneys in the east block.

Oxwich Castle southeast wall showing the top floor 'long gallery' window.

Oxwich Castle dovecote and northeast wing.

Weobley Castle

Weobley has been occupied within living memory, and numerous alterations have been made during its long history. It was built on a strong site with excellent protection on the N. side where there is a natural fall to the salt marshes below. The E. side is protected to a lesser extent, and the most level approach is from the W. It appears that building on the east side was never entirely completed.

The oldest part of the castle appears to be the thick-walled square tower, now only about two metres high but with walls over 2m. thick, which stands on the south side of the courtyard. This tower may date from the mid thirteenth century. In the late thirteenth and early fourteenth centuries, most of the buildings we see today were added around

Weobley Castle and the Burry Estuary.

Weobley Castle interior.

the courtyard. Initially, the great hall was built, and then the wing on the west with private rooms for the lord of the manor.

Weobley has been described both as a castle and as a fortified manor house. However, since its defences were not strong, while its internal domestic arrangements were well developed, Weobley was clearly a well-fortified manor-house. It not a serious fortification for a garrison, although its high crenellated walls would have provided a good measure of security for its occupants. Various illustrious owners included the de la Bere family, Sir Rhys ap Thomas, and members of the Herbert and Mansel families. The building was severely damaged in Owain Glyndŵr's rising (*c.*1403), but continued in use as a dwelling, as the inserted windows of Tudor style confirm.

In the eighteenth century, the hall block was converted into a farm-house, but by 1920, most modifications had been cleared and re-roofing done. There are substantial traces of an extensive late-medieval barn, measuring more than 45m. x 9m., among the private farm buildings immediately east of the castle. Its walls average more than a metre in thickness. Vestiges of a limekiln, found near the S.E. tower, may have been in use in the early fourteenth century.

Weobley Castle from the estuary.

Loughor Castle

The first castle at Loughor was built on the line of a Roman road and in the south-east corner of a long-derelict Roman fort. The site is a naturally strong one, standing on a narrow and steep-sided gravel promontory dominating the ford and ferry giving access to Gower from the west, as Swansea Castle commanded the access from the east.

It consisted of a great mound of clay and rubble with a rampart of similar material around its crest. Early records of its destruction in the twelfth century, when it was burnt by the Welsh in 1151, were again confirmed by excavations in 1969, which revealed extensive areas of burning on the top of the mound. After a short abandonment, the defences were repaired, this time with a laid stone wall as a rampart. In the late thirteenth century, a simple rectangular stone tower was added at one side of the mound, and most of this still stands. This appears to have been for purely residential purposes and was built over the scarp which fell from the motte-like mound. To accompany this, there was in-filling of the interior of the first castle ring-work.

Loughor Castle mound.

Loughor Castle chimney place.

Loughor Castle walls.

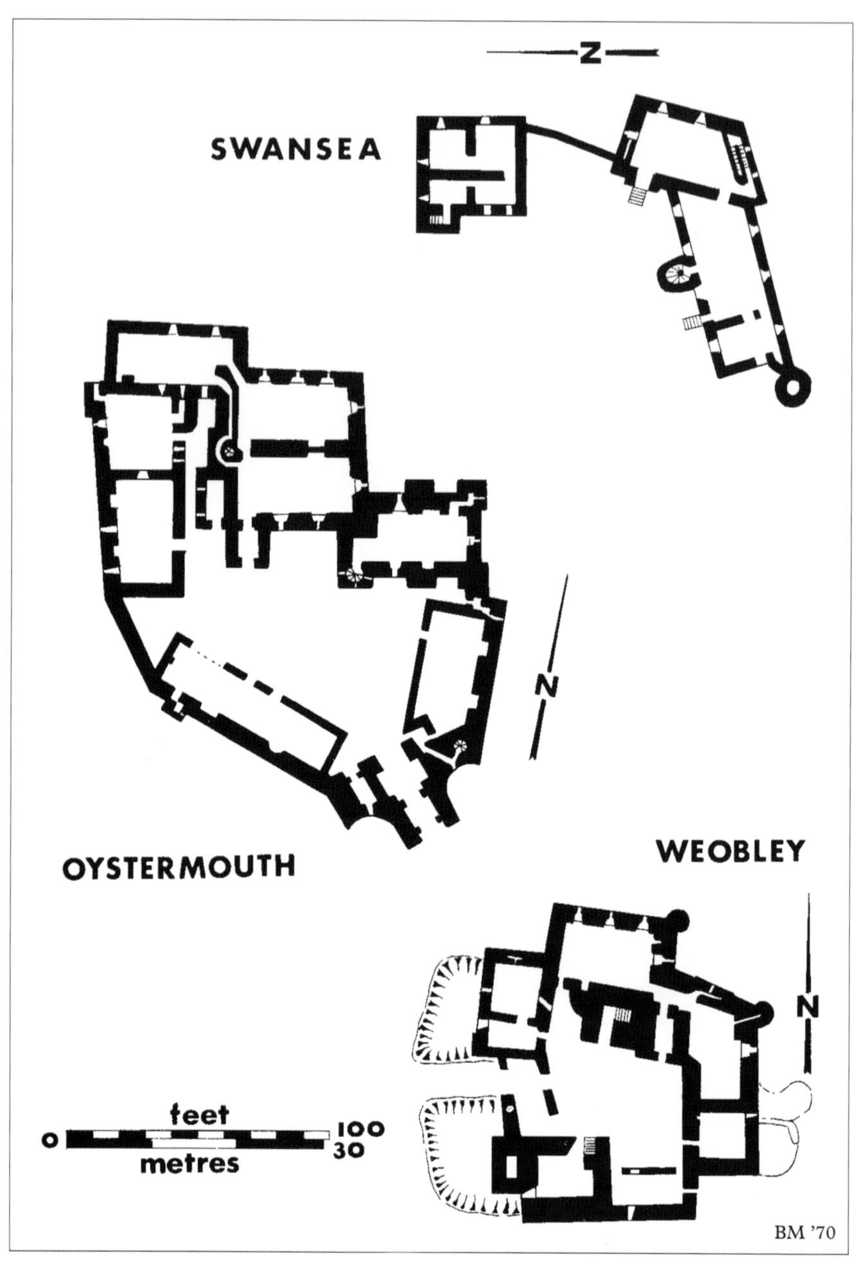

Plans of Gower Castles . . .

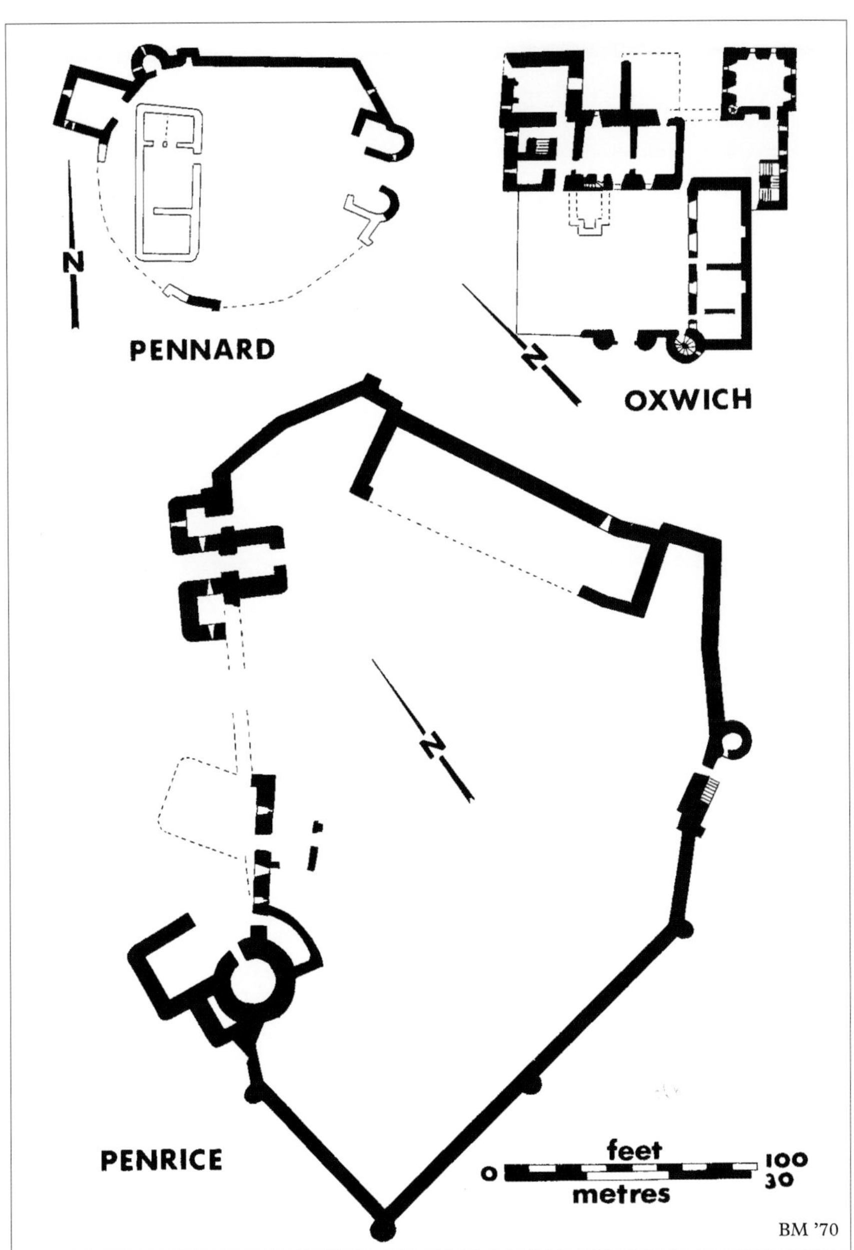

. . . all to one scale.

27

The crest of Sir Rice Mansell, 1487-1559.
Over the gate of Oxwich Castle.

ACCESS TO GOWER CASTLES

Penrice Castle, Landimore, Barland and Penrice Old Castle (the "Mounty Bank"), being privately owned are not open to the public, but each can be viewed, at a distance, from a public footpath or road. Swansea Castle (Cadw) can be viewed at close quarters from the lawned landscaped area fronting Castle Street and from The Strand. Loughor (Cadw), Pennard (Pennard Golf Club) and Penmaen (National Trust) can be freely visited; Weobley (Cadw), Oxwich (Cadw) and Oystermouth (City & County of Swansea, assisted by the Friends of Oystermouth Castle) are subject to opening times and entry fees.

Front cover: Weobley Castle.
Back cover: view over the saltmarshes, looking east from Weobley Castle.